THE
MULTI COOKER
COOKBOOK

www.cookbookdesigner.com

Printed in the U.S.A.

Acknowledgements

We would like to thank our families for all their support and patience during the process of putting this cookbook together.

A very special thanks to Wolfgang Puck. It is an honor and a privilege to be associated with such an amazing chef. Thank you for your guidance, professionalism and patience. Your support over the years has inspired both of us to provide our customers with the best products possible.

Our deepest thanks to the entire WP team: Sydney Silverman, Arnie Simon, Jonathan Schwartz, Mike Sanseverino, Phoebe Soong and Nicolle Brown. We are very fortunate to work with the best in the business. Thank you for giving us this tremendous opportunity of writing cookbooks.

Thank you to the outstanding people behind the scenes. This cookbook would not be possible without your hard work and dedication. Thanks to Daniel Koren, Chris Davis, Tracy Ferguson, Nevar Murray, Mike Alberts, Julie Edwards and Greg Getz.

We would also like to thank everyone at HSN and TSC for your support. You have created an outlet where we can express ourselves and have the ability to touch millions of people with our cookbooks.

Thank you to our HSN and TSC viewers. Your support over the years is greatly appreciated. Thanks for all the suggestions that help us make our cookbooks better. You are the reason we do what we do.

Marian   Debbie Meenay

Debra Murray and Marian Getz have been my assistants at the Home Shopping Network for many years. Their passion for good cooking and quality appliances has helped many people become better cooks. The multi cooker is quickly becoming one of their favorite kitchen tools. I have urged them to share their favorite recipes and knowledge about the multi cooker with as many people as possible through this cookbook.

Debra Murray certainly knows how to take advantage of the multi cooker. She combines high quality, seasonal, locally grown ingredients to make easy, delicious and effortless meals in no time. The multi cooker makes it possible to enjoy all types of cuisines. Most importantly, in this age of two-career couples, where many families find it difficult to put a home-cooked dinner on the table each evening, Debra shows us how the multi cooker can allow us to do just that.

Marian Getz has taken her years of being a mother, wife as well as a chef and transferred her love for cooking into these recipes. So many of her recipes are easy to prepare, very economical and taste great. As long as I have known Marian, she continues to cook with passion and understands the importance of sharing her knowledge and experience with others.

Both Debra and Marian are talented cooks in their own right and share my WELL (Wolfgang's Eat, Love, Live!™) philosophy of good cooking and warm hospitality. I believe everyone should use the freshest, all-natural ingredients, food that is locally grown, organic whenever possible and raised using sustainable humane methods.

As I learned long ago, alongside my mother and grandmother, you should always put lots of love into everything you cook. This is certainly evident in this collection of Deb and Marian's multi cooker recipes.

Wolfgang Puck

Entrees

Sweets

Extras

TEN COOKING TIPS

1. Making A Weekly Menu

Take time to plan your menu for the upcoming week. Plan menus for breakfast, lunch, dinner and even the kid's lunches. Doing this will save you time and money. It does take some time to do, but get the whole family involved and turn it into something fun.

2. Shop The Ads

Scanning through the weekly ads of your local grocery store and cutting coupons will help you save money. Also, many grocery stores put coupons on their websites that can be printed. For the tech savy, some stores even have apps for smart phones which will let you sync your shopping list and coupons from your computer to your cell phone.

3. Make A Grocery List

Having a list of what you need before you go to the store is one of the best ways to save money. The list should be based on your weekly menu in combination with the weekly sales and coupons from your grocery store to get the most for your money. Going to the store without a grocery list will cause impulse buying of items you don't really need.

4. Buy In Bulk When Possible

If you have a large club store in your area, get a membership. Buying in bulk is a great way to save money. However, you need to be smart when buying in bulk. Are you really going to use 50 pounds of onions or 15 dozen eggs? Purchasing meats in bulk is smart. Use what you need and freeze the rest. It's like building a treasure chest inside your freezer.

5. Have All Ingredients Ready

Gather all the ingredients that a recipe calls for before you begin cooking. Place everything on the left side of the counter. When you have added something to the pot, transfer it to the right side. This way if you get distracted, you will know where you left off.

6. Multi-Tasking

Planning the meal before you start cooking will ensure that everything will be ready at the same time. For example, while the rice is cooking, prepare the salad. The delay function of the multi cooker will assist you with multi-tasking as well.

7. Make A One-Pot-Meal

Marian likes to say "everybody goes in the pool at the same time." A one-pot-meal is wonderful for those busy days. One-Pot-Meals require less cleanup and are so easy to make. There are several one-pot-meals in this book or create one of your own.

8. Cook Once - Eat Twice/Prep Once - Use Twice

Things like chili and pasta sauce can be frozen for use later. Take advantage of the volume the multi cooker can make and save the remainder for later in the week. Also, prep for more than you need today. Look at the weekly menu and determine if you will need some of today's prepped ingredients later. For example, if you're chopping onions for today's meal, can you use onions later in the week? If so, prep extra today and use it later.

9. Layers Of Flavor

One of the secrets to great tasting food is layers of flavor. That's why chefs add salt, sugar, vinegar or pepper...or all of the above. When cooking in the multi cooker and the recipe calls for water, use stock or bases instead. If you're making chicken noodle casserole, cook the pasta in chicken stock instead of water for a tremendous boost in flavor. Bases are concentrated pastes that dissolve when added to water. Chicken and beef bases are the most popular flavors.

10. Tis The Season

When possible, cook with the foods that are in season. The produce department in your grocery store will showcase the fruits and vegetables as they come into season. They often even offer them on sale. Buy meats in bulk when they go on sale and don't shy away from the cheaper cuts of meat. While they tend to be tougher, slow cooking them in the multi cooker makes them tender and taste even better.

PANTRY TIPS

PANTRY TIPS

Being prepared to cook the recipes in this book, or any recipe for that matter, is one of the keys to success in the kitchen. Your pantry must be stocked with the basics. We all know how frustrating it can be when you go to the cupboard and what you need is not there. This list includes some of the ingredients you will find in this book and some that we feel are important to always have on hand.

Perishables:

Onions
Garlic
Tomatoes
Carrots
Celery
Ginger
Bell Peppers
White Potatoes
Sweet Potatoes
Squashes
Citrus
Apples
Bananas
Lettuce
Spinach
Fresh Herbs
Green Onions
Milk
Cream Cheese
Parmesan Cheese
Yogurt
Other Cheeses You Like

Spices:

Kosher Salt
Pepper
Bay Leaves
Sage
Oregano
Thyme
Chili Flakes
Cumin Seeds
Curry Powder
Onion Powder
Garlic Powder
Dry Mustard
Ground Cinnamon
Nutmeg
Cloves
Chili Powder

Dry goods:

Oils
Vinegar
Honey
Sugars
Sugar Substitute
Vanilla
Extracts/Flavorings
Agave Syrup
Canned Tomatoes
Canned Beans
Canned Vegetables
Dried Chilies
Pasta
Lentils
Stocks
Powdered Bouillon
Olives
Ketchup
Mustard
Pickles

It is not necessary to have all the items listed at all times. However, if you are feeling creative, adventurous or just following a recipe, it's great to have a good selection in the kitchen.

VEGETABLE SOUP

Makes 4 to 6 servings

Ingredients:

2 tablespoons extra-virgin olive oil

1 medium onion, diced

2 celery stalks, sliced

2 garlic cloves, minced

1 cup cabbage, shredded

1 teaspoon sea salt

½ teaspoon freshly ground pepper

4 cups vegetable stock

1 can (14 ounces) petite diced tomatoes

2 cups frozen mixed vegetables

1 sprig of fresh thyme

Method:

1. *Pour oil into the multi cooker; set to WHITE and heat oil for 2 minutes.*
2. *Add onions and celery to the multi cooker; cook for 5 minutes.*
3. *Add garlic, cabbage, salt and pepper to the multi cooker.*
4. *Secure lid and cook for an additional 5 minutes.*
5. *Add remaining ingredients to the multi cooker; stir.*
6. *Secure lid and cook for an additional 20 minutes.*
7. *Remove thyme, cook for an additional 5 minutes and serve.*

TIP
For a heartier soup, add a cup of dry pasta during the last 15 minutes of cooking.

DON'S CHILI

Makes 4 to 6 servings

Ingredients:

1 pound ground chicken

1 medium onion, chopped

2 garlic cloves, chopped

3 tablespoons chili seasoning mix

1 tablespoon ground cumin

1 jar (28 ounces) spaghetti sauce

2 cups water

1 cup frozen corn

Method:

1. *Place the chicken into the multi cooker and break it apart using a wooden spoon.*
2. *Add the onions and garlic to the multi cooker.*
3. *Set to WHITE and cook for 10 minutes.*
4. *Drain the liquid from the chicken mixture using a strainer.*
5. *Place the chicken mixture back into the multi cooker.*
6. *Add remaining ingredients to the multi cooker and stir.*
7. *Secure lid and cook for an additional 25 minutes.*
8. *Serve immediately.*

TIP

You can substitute ground turkey, ground beef or even ground bison for the chicken in this recipe.

3 BEAN VEGETARIAN CHILI

Makes 6 to 8 servings

Ingredients:

1 tablespoon extra-virgin olive oil

1 medium onion, chopped

1 red bell pepper, diced

2 garlic cloves, minced

1 teaspoon ground cumin

1 teaspoon salt

½ teaspoon freshly ground pepper

2 chipotle peppers in adobo sauce, seeded and chopped

1 can (15 ounces) black beans, drained

1 can (15 ounces) light red kidney beans, drained

1 can (15 ounces) garbanzo beans, drained

1 cup frozen corn

1 can (14 ounces) petite diced tomatoes

Method:

1. *Pour oil into the multi cooker; set to WHITE and heat oil for 2 minutes.*
2. *Add the onions to the multi cooker.*
3. *Secure lid and cook for 5 minutes.*
4. *Add remaining ingredients to the multi cooker; stir.*
5. *Secure lid and cook for an additional 30 minutes.*
6. *Serve immediately.*

TIP

Serve topped with sour cream, cilantro, chopped red onions and shredded Cheddar cheese.

MANHATTAN CLAM CHOWDER

Makes 4 to 6 servings

Ingredients:

1 tablespoon extra-virgin olive oil

4 turkey bacon strips, chopped

1 medium onion, chopped

½ teaspoon salt

½ teaspoon freshly ground pepper

2 celery stalks, chopped

2 carrots, peeled and chopped

1 Yukon Gold potato, peeled and diced

1 can (14 ounces) petite diced tomatoes

2 cans (6.5 ounces each) chopped clams in juice

1 cup clamato juice

2 cups chicken stock

1 tablespoon fresh parsley, chopped

Method:

1. *Pour oil into the multi cooker; set to WHITE and heat oil for 2 minutes.*

2. *Add the turkey bacon to the multi cooker.*

3. *Secure lid and cook for 5 minutes.*

4. *Add the onions, secure lid and cook for an additional 5 minutes.*

5. *Add remaining ingredients, except parsley, to the multi cooker; stir.*

6. *Secure lid and cook for an additional 30 minutes.*

7. *Top with parsley and serve.*

TIP

This tomato based chowder has far fewer calories than the cream based New England variety.

NAVY BEAN SOUP

Makes 4 to 6 servings

SOUPS & STEWS

Ingredients:

1 tablespoon extra-virgin olive oil

1 medium onion, chopped

2 celery stalks, chopped

1 carrot, peeled and chopped

1 medium potato, peeled and diced

1 pound dry navy beans, rinsed

5 cups chicken stock

1 smoked turkey wing

½ teaspoon salt

½ teaspoon freshly ground pepper

½ teaspoon sugar

1 sprig fresh thyme

Method:

1. *Pour oil into the multi cooker; set to WHITE and heat oil for 2 minutes.*
2. *Add the onions, celery, carrots and potatoes to the multi cooker.*
3. *Secure lid and cook for 5 minutes.*
4. *Add remaining ingredients to the multi cooker; stir.*
5. *Secure lid and cook for an additional hour or until the beans are tender.*
6. *Remove the meat from the turkey wing.*
7. *Place the meat back into the multi cooker and discard the bone.*
8. *Remove thyme and serve.*

TIP

Serve with a crusty baguette
and a green salad
to make a complete meal.

SPLIT PEA SOUP

Makes 8 servings

Ingredients:

2 tablespoons extra-virgin olive oil

2 medium onions, chopped

2 teaspoons salt

1 teaspoon freshly ground pepper

2 celery stalks, chopped

2 carrots, peeled and chopped

1 cup smoked turkey sausage, sliced

2 cups dried split peas, rinsed

8 cups chicken stock

4 basil leaves, chopped

Method:

1. *Pour oil into the multi cooker; set to WHITE and heat oil for 2 minutes.*
2. *Add the onions, salt and pepper to the multi cooker; cook for 5 minutes.*
3. *Add the celery and carrots to the multi cooker; cook for 5 minutes.*
4. *Add remaining ingredients, except basil, to the multi cooker; stir then secure lid.*
5. *Cook for an additional 45 minutes or until peas are tender.*
6. *Top with basil and serve.*

TIP

Finish the soup
with a drizzle of
red wine vinegar.

LENTIL SOUP

Makes 8 servings

Ingredients:

4 cups lentils, rinsed

8 cups vegetable stock

4 celery stalks, thinly sliced

2 large carrots, peeled and thinly sliced

2 cans (14 ounces each) stewed tomatoes with onions and garlic

10 button mushrooms, sliced

1 teaspoon salt

1 teaspoon freshly ground pepper

1 teaspoon lemon juice

2 teaspoons fresh parsley, chopped

2 bay leaves

Method:

1. *Place all ingredients into the multi cooker; stir then secure lid.*
2. *Set to WHITE and cook for 25 minutes or until lentils are tender.*
3. *Discard the bay leaves and serve.*

TIP

Since lentils cook fast,
keep a variety of them in your pantry
for a quick, nutritious meal.

THAI STYLE COCONUT SOUP

Makes 4 to 6 servings

Ingredients:

1 teaspoon sesame oil

1 small onion, chopped

1 garlic clove, minced

1 teaspoon fresh ginger, grated

1 teaspoon minced lemongrass (optional)

1 teaspoon red curry paste

1 can (13.5 ounces) light coconut milk

2 cups chicken stock

1 tablespoon brown sugar

1 can (8 ounces) bean sprouts, drained

½ Serrano pepper, diced

1 red bell pepper, julienned

½ cup canned straw mushrooms, drained

2 cups cooked chicken, shredded

1 lime, juice and zest

1 teaspoon soy sauce

¼ cup fresh cilantro leaves, chopped

Method:

1. *Pour oil into the multi cooker; set to WHITE and heat oil for 2 minutes.*
2. *Add the onions, garlic, ginger and lemongrass to the multi cooker.*
3. *Secure lid and cook for 5 minutes.*
4. *Add the red curry paste to the multi cooker; stir.*
5. *Add remaining ingredients, except cilantro, to the multi cooker.*
6. *Secure lid and cook for an additional 10 minutes.*
7. *Top with cilantro and serve.*

TIP
You can substitute shrimp for the chicken.

BEET SOUP

Makes 6 to 8 servings

Ingredients:

1 tablespoon extra-virgin olive oil

1 medium onion, chopped

1 celery stalk, chopped

2 beets, washed, peeled and sliced

2 carrots, peeled and sliced

½ cup cabbage, shredded

1 small turnip, peeled and diced

4 cups beef stock

1 can (14 ounces) petite diced tomatoes

½ teaspoon salt

½ teaspoon freshly ground pepper

1 sprig fresh thyme

Method:

1. *Pour oil into the multi cooker; set to WHITE and heat oil for 2 minutes.*
2. *Add the onions to the multi cooker.*
3. *Secure lid and cook for 5 minutes.*
4. *Add remaining ingredients to the multi cooker; stir.*
5. *Secure lid and cook for an additional 45 minutes.*
6. *Discard the thyme and serve hot or cold.*

TIP
This soup is amazing topped with a dollop of sour cream.

ESCAROLE BEAN SOUP

Makes 4 to 6 servings

Ingredients:

1 tablespoon extra-virgin olive oil

1 shallot, minced

3 garlic cloves, minced

1 pound smoked turkey sausage, thinly sliced

1 escarole head, washed and chopped

1 can (15 ounces) cannellini beans, drained

1 sprig fresh thyme

4 cups chicken stock

2 tablespoons Parmesan cheese, grated

½ teaspoon salt

½ teaspoon freshly ground pepper

Method:

1. *Pour oil into the multi cooker; set to STEAM and timer to 30 minutes.*
2. *Heat oil for 2 minutes then add the shallots, garlic and sausage.*
3. *Secure lid and cook for 5 minutes.*
4. *Add remaining ingredients to the multi cooker; stir.*
5. *Secure lid and cook for 20 minutes.*
6. *Remove thyme and serve.*

MOROCCAN VEGETABLE STEW

Makes 4 to 6 servings

SOUPS & STEWS

Ingredients:

1 tablespoon extra-virgin olive oil

1 medium onion, chopped

1 turnip, peeled and diced

1 medium eggplant, peeled and diced

1 sweet potato, peeled and diced

1 medium Russet potato, peeled and diced

1 teaspoon salt

½ teaspoon ground ginger

1 teaspoon paprika

1 teaspoon ground cumin

¼ teaspoon ground cinnamon

4 saffron strands

1 can (14 ounces) petite diced tomatoes

¼ cup dried fruit, chopped

1 Preserved Lemon (see recipe on page 136)

1 cup vegetable stock

1 teaspoon flat leaf parsley, chopped

Method:

1. *Pour oil into the multi cooker; set to STEAM and timer to 30 minutes.*
2. *Heat oil for 2 minutes then add the onions to the multi cooker.*
3. *Secure lid and cook for 5 minutes.*
4. *Add remaining ingredients, except parsley, to the multi cooker; stir.*
5. *Secure lid and cook for 20 minutes or until the vegetables are tender.*
6. *Top with parsley and serve.*

TIP
My favorite dried fruits
to use for this recipe are
apricots and prunes.

OLD FASHIONED BEEF STEW

Makes 4 servings

Ingredients:

2 tablespoons canola oil

1 pound beef chuck, cut into 1½-inch cubes

Kosher salt and pepper to taste

½ cup red wine or water

5 cups beef stock

¼ cup ketchup

1 tablespoon Worcestershire sauce

2 teaspoons soy sauce

1 bay leaf

2 large yellow onions, cubed

2 garlic cloves, minced

3 Russet potatoes, cubed

3 carrots, peeled and cubed

3 celery stalks, cubed

2 tablespoons quick-cook tapioca

Method:

1. *Preheat oil in a large skillet over medium-high heat.*
2. *When oil is hot, add the beef cubes in a single layer.*
3. *Season with salt and pepper then brown the meat on all sides.*
4. *Transfer the meat to the multi cooker.*
5. *To deglaze the skillet, add the wine or water to the skillet and scrape up all the brown bits from the bottom of the pan then transfer to the multi cooker.*
6. *Add remaining ingredients to the multi cooker; stir gently then secure lid.*
7. *Set to SLOW COOK and timer to 5 hours.*
8. *When multi cooker switches to KEEP WARM, skim off excess fat from the surface.*
9. *Discard the bay leaf and adjust the seasoning if necessary.*
10. *Serve hot.*

TIP

To stretch this stew even further, add extra vegetables such as corn or green beans and serve over hot cooked egg noodles.

CAULIFLOWER CHICKPEA STEW

Makes 6 servings

Ingredients:

2 tablespoons coconut oil

2½ cups onions, chopped

1 teaspoon salt

½ teaspoon freshly ground pepper

5 teaspoons curry powder

6 cups cauliflower florets

2 cans (15½ ounces each) garbanzo beans, drained

2 cans (10 ounces each) diced tomatoes with green chilies

1 can (13½ ounces) light coconut milk

4 cups vegetable stock

½ cup fresh cilantro, chopped

Method:

1. *Pour oil into the multi cooker; set to STEAM and timer to 30 minutes.*
2. *Heat oil for 2 minutes then add the onions to the multi cooker.*
3. *Season with salt and pepper.*
4. *Secure lid and cook for 5 minutes.*
5. *Add the curry powder to the multi cooker and stir.*
6. *Add the cauliflower and beans to the multi cooker; stir for 1 minute.*
7. *Add the tomatoes, coconut milk and stock to the multi cooker; stir.*
8. *Secure lid and cook for 15 minutes, stirring occasionally.*
9. *Stir in the cilantro and serve.*

TIP
This is delicious served with couscous.

SCRAMBLED EGGS

Makes 4 servings

Ingredients:

6 large eggs
¼ cup half & half
½ teaspoon salt
¼ teaspoon freshly ground pepper

Method:

1. *Secure the lid of the multi cooker; set to STEAM and timer to 15 minutes.*
2. *In a large bowl, combine all ingredients; whisk well.*
3. *Apply non-stick spray to the inside of the multi cooker.*
4. *When multi cooker is hot, add the egg mixture.*
5. *Secure lid and cook for 1 minute.*
6. *Scramble the eggs using a rubber spatula.*
7. *Secure lid and cook for 1 additional minute.*
8. *Serve immediately.*

TIP
Add your favorite shredded cheese before cooking.

ZUCCHINI FRITTATA

Makes 4 to 6 servings

Ingredients:

2 zucchini, shredded

2 green onions, chopped

1 cup mozzarella cheese, shredded

8 large eggs, beaten

1 teaspoon salt

½ teaspoon freshly ground pepper

½ cup heavy cream

1 large tomato, diced

1 teaspoon fresh basil, chopped

Method:

1. *Secure the lid of the multi cooker; set to STEAM and timer to 30 minutes.*
2. *In a large bowl, combine all ingredients, except tomatoes and basil; mix well.*
3. *Apply non-stick spray to the inside of the multi cooker.*
4. *Pour the mixture into the multi cooker.*
5. *Secure lid and cook for 15 minutes.*
6. *Stir ingredients using a silicone spatula; secure lid.*
7. *Cooking is complete when the center of the frittata is firm to the touch.*
8. *Serve topped with tomatoes and basil.*

LOW-FAT SPINACH STRATA

Makes 6 servings

Ingredients:

1 cup egg substitute

2 cups low-fat milk

¼ teaspoon dried thyme

¼ teaspoon salt

¼ teaspoon coarsely ground black pepper

Pinch of ground nutmeg

1 package (10 ounces) frozen chopped spinach, thawed and drained

1 cup low-fat mozzarella cheese, shredded

8 slices whole grain bread, cut into ¾-inch pieces

Method:

1. *In a large bowl, combine egg substitute, milk, thyme, salt, pepper and nutmeg; stir.*
2. *Add remaining ingredients to the bowl; stir using a rubber spatula.*
3. *Pour the mixture into the multi cooker.*
4. *Secure lid, set to STEAM and timer to 30 minutes.*
5. *When cooking is complete, let rest on KEEP WARM for 20 minutes then serve.*

TIP

Top the strata
with some diced tomatoes,
basil and olive oil.

FIESTA TABBOULEH

Makes 4 to 6 servings

Ingredients:

1 cup bulgur, rinsed

2½ cups vegetable stock

½ teaspoon cumin seeds

1 pint grape tomatoes, chopped

2 green onions, chopped

1 garlic clove, minced

1 tomatillo, finely chopped

2 tablespoons fresh cilantro, chopped

1 Serrano pepper, seeds and membrane removed, minced

1 red bell pepper, diced

1 teaspoon sea salt

½ teaspoon freshly ground pepper

1 lime, juice and zest

Method:

1. *Place the bulgur, stock and cumin seeds into the multi cooker.*
2. *Secure lid and set to WHITE.*
3. *Cooking is complete when multi cooker switches to KEEP WARM.*
4. *In a bowl, combine remaining ingredients; toss well.*
5. *Add the bulgur mixture to the bowl, toss and refrigerate for 2 hours.*
6. *Serve chilled.*

TIP

This goes great with any grilled meat or even a store-bought rotisserie chicken.

QUINOA TABBOULEH

Makes 4 to 6 servings

Ingredients:

1 cup quinoa, rinsed

1¼ cups water

1 teaspoon salt

1 cup grape tomatoes, diced

1 tablespoon flat leaf parsley, finely chopped

1 tablespoon mint, finely chopped

6 green onions, finely sliced

6 tablespoons extra-virgin olive oil

2 tablespoons fresh lemon juice

½ teaspoon freshly ground pepper

Method:

1. *Place quinoa, water and salt into the multi cooker; secure lid.*
2. *Set to WHITE and cook until the multi cooker switches to KEEP WARM.*
3. *Transfer the quinoa to a bowl and let cool.*
4. *Add remaining ingredients to the bowl, stir and serve.*

GARBANZO BEANS & RICE SALAD

Makes 6 servings

Ingredients:

1 cup short grain brown rice, rinsed

2¼ cups chicken stock

1 cup garbanzo beans, cooked

1 carrot, peeled and sliced

2 green onions, chopped

2 celery stalks, sliced

1 zucchini, thinly sliced

1 yellow bell pepper, chopped

Dressing:

1 teaspoon red wine vinegar

1 teaspoon lemon juice

½ teaspoon salt

3 basil leaves

½ teaspoon prepared mustard

2 tablespoons extra-virgin olive oil

Method:

1. *Place the rice and stock into the multi cooker.*
2. *Secure lid and set to BROWN.*
3. *While rice is cooking, combine all dressing ingredients in a bowl.*
4. *Whisk dressing until smooth then set aside.*
5. *When multi cooker switches to KEEP WARM, transfer the rice to a large bowl.*
6. *Add remaining ingredients and dressing to the bowl; toss well.*
7. *Cover and chill for 2 hours before serving.*

VEGGIE FRIED RICE

Makes 6 servings

Ingredients:

2 cups brown basmati rice, rinsed

4 cups vegetable stock

2 teaspoons soy sauce

1 teaspoon miso paste

2 teaspoons sesame oil

2 garlic cloves, minced

1 teaspoon ginger, grated

1 can (8 ounces) bean sprouts, drained

2 cups frozen Asian vegetable blend

½ cup egg substitute

2 green onions, sliced

Method:

1. *Place the rice, stock, soy sauce and miso paste into the multi cooker.*
2. *Secure lid and set to BROWN.*
3. *When multi cooker switches to KEEP WARM, transfer the rice to a large bowl then set aside.*
4. *Add the oil, garlic and ginger to the multi cooker.*
5. *Set to STEAM, timer to 20 minutes and cook for 5 minutes.*
6. *Add the bean sprouts and Asian vegetables to the multi cooker.*
7. *Secure lid and cook for 5 minutes.*
8. *Add the egg substitute to the multi cooker.*
9. *Scramble the mixture using a rubber spatula.*
10. *Add the rice back into the multi cooker and stir well.*
11. *Secure lid and cook for an additional 10 minutes.*
12. *Top with green onions and serve.*

TIP
You can find miso paste in Asian markets or health food stores.

MEDITERRANEAN RICE

Makes 4 to 6 servings

Ingredients:

1 tablespoon extra-virgin olive oil

1 small onion, diced

2 garlic cloves, minced

1 roasted red pepper, diced

1 large zucchini, diced

1 large eggplant, peeled and diced

½ teaspoon salt

½ teaspoon freshly ground pepper

½ teaspoon dry oregano

2 cups long grain rice, rinsed

½ cup white wine

1 can (14 ounces) stewed tomatoes with peppers

2 cups vegetable stock

¼ cup feta cheese, crumbled

Method:

1. *Pour oil into the multi cooker; set to WHITE and heat oil for 2 minutes.*
2. *Add the onions to the multi cooker; secure lid and cook for 5 minutes.*
3. *Add remaining ingredients, except feta cheese, to the multi cooker; stir.*
4. *Secure lid and cook until the multi cooker switches to KEEP WARM.*
5. *Stir and serve topped with feta cheese.*

VEGETABLE
COUSCOUS

Makes 4 servings

Ingredients:

1 tablespoon extra-virgin olive oil

1 shallot, minced

½ cup zucchini, diced

½ cup canned northern white beans, drained

1 can (14 ounces) petite diced tomatoes with garlic

¾ cup vegetable stock

1 box (5.4 ounces) quick-cook couscous (cooks in 5 minutes)

1 tablespoon fresh parsley, chopped

Method:

1. *Pour oil into the multi cooker; set to WHITE and heat oil for 2 minutes.*
2. *Add the shallots to the multi cooker; secure lid and cook for 5 minutes.*
3. *Add remaining ingredients, except parsley, to the multi cooker; stir.*
4. *Secure lid and cook until the multi cooker switches to KEEP WARM.*
5. *Stir in the parsley and serve.*

GINGERED BRUSSELS
SPROUTS & RICE

Makes 4 servings

Ingredients:

2 tablespoons teriyaki sauce

1 tablespoon ginger, grated

1 green onion, chopped

3 garlic cloves, minced

1½ pounds brussels sprouts, washed and bottoms trimmed

1 red bell pepper, julienned

2 cups jasmine rice, rinsed

2 cups water

1 teaspoon salt

Method:

1. *In a bowl, combine teriyaki sauce, ginger, onions and garlic.*
2. *Add the sprouts and peppers to the bowl; toss and let marinate for 30 minutes.*
3. *Place remaining ingredients into the multi cooker.*
4. *Fit the multi cooker with the steamer basket.*
5. *Add the sprout mixture to the steamer basket; secure lid.*
6. *Set to STEAM and timer to 10 minutes.*
7. *When cooking is complete, serve immediately.*

RED CABBAGE

Makes 4 to 6 servings

Ingredients:

2 tablespoons extra-virgin olive oil

4 turkey bacon slices, chopped

1 medium onion, thinly sliced

2 Granny Smith apples, peeled, cored and sliced

1 teaspoon salt

½ teaspoon freshly ground pepper

1 head purple cabbage, thinly sliced

1 cup chicken stock

¼ cup apple cider vinegar

½ cup sugar

1 teaspoon apple pie spice

½ cup port wine

¼ cup balsamic vinegar

Method:

1. *Pour oil into the multi cooker; set to STEAM and timer to 20 minutes.*
2. *Heat oil for 2 minutes then add the turkey bacon to the multi cooker.*
3. *Secure lid and cook for 5 minutes.*
4. *Add the onions to the multi cooker.*
5. *Secure lid and cook for an additional 5 minutes.*
6. *Add remaining ingredients to the multi cooker.*
7. *Secure lid and cook until tender.*
8. *Serve immediately.*

STEAMED ARTICHOKES

Makes 4 servings

Artichoke Ingredients:

4 medium-size artichokes

2 teaspoons kosher salt

2 cups water

2 lemons, sliced and divided

Garlic Dipping Sauce:

½ cup good quality mayonnaise

2 garlic cloves, finely minced

1 teaspoon capers, finely minced

1 tablespoon fresh lemon juice

Pinch of kosher salt

Method:

1. *Trim artichokes by using kitchen shears to trim off pointy ends of outer leaves.*
2. *Trim the bottom stem of each artichoke.*
3. *Place artichokes into the multi cooker.*
4. *Add the salt, water and half of the lemon slices.*
5. *Secure lid, set to STEAM and timer to 30 minutes.*
6. *When multi cooker switches to KEEP WARM, test the artichokes for doneness. The leaves should pull off easily. If they need additional time, reset the multi cooker to STEAM and set timer to 10 minutes.*
7. *In a small bowl, combine sauce ingredients; stir well.*
8. *Serve artichokes with the sauce and remaining lemon slices for dipping.*

TIP

During steaming, keep the lemon slices on top of the artichokes or they will make the water bitter which will make the artichokes too bitter.

ZUCCHINI & TOMATO MEDLEY

Makes 6 to 8 servings

Ingredients:

1 tablespoon olive oil

6 garlic cloves, sliced

1 large yellow onion, sliced

10 medium zucchini, sliced into half-circles

3 cans (14.5 ounces each) stewed tomatoes

½ teaspoon cayenne pepper

Kosher salt and fresh pepper to taste

Method:

1. *Pour oil into the multi cooker; set to STEAM and timer to 10 minutes.*
2. *When oil is hot, add the garlic and onions to the multi cooker; sauté until fragrant and translucent.*
3. *Add the zucchini and stir to combine; secure lid.*
4. *Switch multi cooker to SLOW COOK and timer to 3 hours.*
5. *Cook until zucchini are very tender.*

TIP

This freezes very well so make batches of it when summer gardens produce an overabundance of zucchini.

STEAMED
VEGETABLES

Makes 6 servings

Ingredients:

1 cup water

1 tablespoon salt

2 tablespoons lemon juice

1 cup broccoli florets

1 cup cauliflower florets

1 cup carrots, peeled and sliced

Method:

1. *Place the water, salt and lemon juice into the multi cooker.*
2. *Fit the multi cooker with the steamer basket.*
3. *Place remaining ingredients into the steamer basket; secure lid.*
4. *Set to STEAM and timer to 8 minutes.*
5. *When cooking is complete, serve immediately.*

TIP
This is delicious topped
with freshly grated
Parmesan cheese.

LOW-FAT MAC & CHEESE

Makes 4 to 6 servings

Ingredients:

3 cups dry elbow pasta

5 cups chicken stock

1 teaspoon salt

1 teaspoon freshly ground pepper

1 package (8 ounces) low-fat cream cheese

½ cup low-fat milk

¾ cup low-fat mozzarella cheese, shredded

¾ cup low-fat Cheddar cheese, shredded

1 cup Parmesan cheese, shredded

Method:

1. *Place the pasta and stock into the multi cooker.*

2. *Secure lid and set to WHITE.*

3. *When multi cooker switches to KEEP WARM, add remaining ingredients.*

4. *Stir until the cheeses are melted.*

5. *Serve immediately.*

PASTA CAPRESE SALAD

Makes 4 servings

Ingredients:

2 cups chicken stock

2 cups dry whole grain rotini pasta

3 garlic cloves, minced

¼ cup sun-dried tomatoes in oil, chopped

1 cup grape tomatoes, quartered

4 ounces fresh buffalo mozzarella cheese, diced

5 fresh basil leaves, chopped

Dressing:

1 tablespoon aged balsamic vinegar

½ teaspoon salt

½ teaspoon freshly ground pepper

2 tablespoons extra-virgin olive oil

Method:

1. *Place the stock, pasta and garlic into the multi cooker.*
2. *Secure lid and set to WHITE.*
3. *While pasta is cooking, place all dressing ingredients into a bowl; whisk well.*
4. *When multi cooker switches to KEEP WARM, transfer the pasta to a bowl.*
5. *Add remaining ingredients and dressing to the bowl; toss well.*
6. *Serve hot or cold.*

MEXICAN
RICE & BEANS

Makes 4 to 6 servings

MEATLESS MAINS

Ingredients:

1 tablespoon extra-virgin olive oil

1 red bell pepper, diced

1 small onion, minced

2 garlic cloves, minced

2 cups chicken stock

2 cups long-grain white rice, rinsed

1 teaspoon ground cumin

1 can (15 ounces) red kidney beans, drained

2 cans (10 ounces each) diced tomatoes with cilantro and lime

2 cups frozen corn

2 tablespoons fresh cilantro leaves, chopped

Method:

1. *Pour oil into the multi cooker; set to WHITE and heat oil for 2 minutes.*
2. *Add the bell peppers and onions to the multi cooker.*
3. *Secure lid and cook for 5 minutes.*
4. *Add the garlic to the multi cooker and cook for 1 additional minute.*
5. *Add the stock and rice to the multi cooker; stir then secure lid.*
6. *When multi cooker switches to KEEP WARM, add remaining ingredients.*
7. *Secure lid and let stand for 10 minutes before serving.*

SPINACH ENCHILADAS

Makes 4 servings

Ingredients:

1 tablespoon extra-virgin olive oil

1 shallot, minced

1 garlic clove, minced

1 package (10 ounces) frozen chopped spinach, thawed and drained

1 teaspoon ground cumin

1 teaspoon salt

½ teaspoon freshly ground pepper

1 package (8 ounces) low-fat cream cheese

1 cup Monterey Jack cheese, shredded

8 whole wheat tortillas

1 cup salsa verde (see page 139)

1 cup low-fat mozzarella cheese, shredded

¼ cup sour cream

1 tablespoon fresh cilantro, chopped

Method:

1. *Pour oil into the multi cooker; set to STEAM and timer to 10 minutes.*
2. *Heat oil for 2 minutes then add the shallots and garlic to the multi cooker.*
3. *Secure lid and cook for 1 minute.*
4. *Add the spinach, cumin, salt and pepper to the multi cooker; stir.*
5. *Secure lid and cook for an additional 5 minutes.*
6. *Add the cream cheese and Monterey Jack cheese; stir until cheeses are melted.*
7. *Place 1/4 cup of cheese mixture onto each tortilla and roll them to form enchiladas.*
8. *Place enchiladas into the multi cooker; top with salsa and mozzarella cheese.*
9. *Secure lid, set to STEAM and timer to 10 minutes.*
10. *When cooking is complete, serve enchiladas topped with sour cream and cilantro.*

VEGETABLE PAELLA

Makes 6 servings

Ingredients:

2 tablespoons extra-virgin olive oil

2 garlic cloves, minced

1 medium onion, minced

3 saffron strands

½ teaspoon turmeric

2 cups jasmine rice, rinsed

2½ cups vegetable stock

1 red bell pepper, julienned

1 cup frozen tiny peas

1 cup canned artichoke hearts, chopped

8 green olives, sliced

3 green onions, chopped

Method:

1. *Pour oil into the multi cooker; set to WHITE and heat oil for 2 minutes.*
2. *Add the garlic and onions to the multi cooker; sauté for 5 minutes.*
3. *Add remaining ingredients, except green onions, to the multi cooker; stir and secure lid.*
4. *Cooking is complete when multi cooker switches to KEEP WARM.*
5. *Serve topped with green onions.*

SUPREME PENNE PASTA

Makes 4 servings

Ingredients:

2 cups vegetable stock

2 cups dry penne pasta

1 can (14 ounces) petite diced tomatoes with garlic and oregano

6 Campari tomatoes, diced

1 cup canned northern white beans, drained

1 cup fresh spinach leaves

¼ cup black olives

6 basil leaves, chopped

Salt and pepper to taste

Method:

1. *Place all ingredients into the multi cooker; stir.*
2. *Secure lid and set to WHITE.*
3. *When multi cooker switches to KEEP WARM, stir and adjust seasoning if desired.*
4. *Serve hot or cold.*

PASTA ALLA PUTTANESCA

Makes 4 servings

Ingredients:

3 cups dry pasta

2 cups chicken stock

2 tablespoons capers

2 Kalamata olives, pitted and sliced

4 anchovy filets

3 garlic cloves, minced

1 can (28 ounces) pear shaped tomatoes in juice, chopped

¼ teaspoon salt

½ teaspoon freshly ground pepper

1 teaspoon fresh oregano leaves, chopped

Method:

1. *Place the pasta, stock, capers, olives, anchovies and garlic into the multi cooker; stir.*
2. *Secure lid and set to WHITE.*
3. *When multi cooker switches to KEEP WARM, add remaining ingredients; secure lid.*
4. *Set to STEAM and timer to 10 minutes.*
5. *When multi cooker switches to KEEP WARM, serve immediately.*

CREAM CHEESE
BROCCOLI PASTA

Makes 4 servings

Ingredients:

2 cups dry whole wheat pasta

2 cups chicken stock

½ teaspoon salt

½ teaspoon freshly ground pepper

½ teaspoon granulated garlic powder

¼ cup low-fat milk

2 ounces low-fat cream cheese

1 cup fresh broccoli florets

¼ cup Parmesan cheese, grated

¼ cup mozzarella cheese, shredded

Method:

1. *Place the pasta, stock, salt, pepper, garlic powder and milk into the multi cooker; stir.*
2. *Secure lid and set to WHITE.*
3. *When multi cooker switches to KEEP WARM, add remaining ingredients; stir well.*
4. *Serve immediately.*

SWISS CHARD PASTA WITH CHICKPEAS

Makes 4 to 6 servings

Ingredients:

2 cups dry whole wheat penne pasta

2 cups chicken stock

2 cups Swiss chard, washed and chopped

2 garlic cloves, minced

1 bay leaf

¼ teaspoon crushed red pepper flakes

1 jar (28 ounces) pasta sauce

1 can (15.5 ounces) chickpeas, drained

1 tablespoon flat leaf parsley, chopped

1 tablespoon Parmesan cheese, grated

Method:

1. *Place the pasta, stock, chard, garlic, bay leaf and pepper flakes into the multi cooker; stir.*
2. *Secure lid and set to WHITE.*
3. *When multi cooker switches to KEEP WARM add remaining ingredients; secure lid.*
4. *Set to STEAM and timer to 10 minutes.*
5. *When cooking is complete, remove bay leaf and serve.*

EASY RATATOUILLE

Makes 4 servings

Ingredients:

1 tablespoon extra-virgin olive oil

1 medium onion, thinly sliced

3 garlic cloves, minced

1 red bell pepper, diced

1 medium eggplant, peeled and diced

1 large zucchini, cut lengthwise then sliced

1 teaspoon salt

½ teaspoon freshly ground pepper

1 can (14 ounces) petite diced tomatoes with basil

1 sprig fresh thyme

Method:

1. *Pour oil into the multi cooker; set to STEAM and timer to 25 minutes.*
2. *When oil is hot, add the onions to the multi cooker; sauté for 5 minutes then add remaining ingredients and stir.*
3. *Secure lid and cook for an additional 15 minutes.*
4. *Serve immediately.*

TIP
This makes a terrific filling for an omelet.

PUMPKIN RISOTTO WITH SAGE

Makes 4 to 6 servings

Ingredients:

2 tablespoons unsalted butter

1 small onion, chopped

1 cup pumpkin, peeled and diced

1 teaspoon salt

½ teaspoon freshly ground pepper

2 cups dry Arborio rice

2 cups chicken stock

½ cup Parmesan cheese, grated

5 fresh sage leaves, chopped

Method:

1. *Place the butter into the multi cooker; set to WHITE and let melt for 2 minutes.*

2. *Add the onions to the multi cooker; secure lid and cook for 5 minutes.*

3. *Add the pumpkin, salt and pepper to the multi cooker.*

4. *Secure lid and cook for an additional 10 minutes.*

5. *Add the rice to the multi cooker; stir until each rice kernel is covered in butter.*

6. *Pour the stock into the multi cooker; secure lid.*

7. *When multi cooker switches to KEEP WARM, stir in remaining ingredients.*

8. *Secure lid and let stand for 5 minutes before serving.*

TIP

You can use canned pumpkin instead of the fresh.

TURKEY MEATBALLS

Makes 4 to 6 servings

Ingredients:

2 tablespoons extra-virgin olive oil

1 small onion, minced

2 garlic cloves, minced

¼ cup whole wheat breadcrumbs

½ cup egg substitute

¼ cup Parmesan cheese, grated

¼ cup flat-leaf parsley, chopped

1 teaspoon salt

½ teaspoon freshly ground black pepper

1 pound ground turkey

1 can (14 ounces) diced tomatoes

2 cups chicken stock

3 cups pasta sauce

Method:

1. *Pour oil into the multi cooker; set to WHITE and heat oil for 2 minutes.*
2. *Add the onions and garlic to the multi cooker; secure lid and cook for 5 minutes.*
3. *Transfer the onion mixture to a bowl and let cool.*
4. *In a separate bowl, combine the breadcrumbs, egg substitute, cheese, parsley, salt and pepper.*
5. *Add the onion mixture and turkey to the bowl and mix well using your hands.*
6. *Form the turkey mixture into golf ball sized meatballs.*
7. *Place the tomatoes and stock into the multi cooker; secure lid.*
8. *Set to WHITE and cook until the liquid comes to a boil.*
9. *Add the meatballs to the multi cooker.*
10. *Secure lid and let the meatballs cook for 1 hour, stirring occasionally.*
11. *Add the pasta sauce to the multi cooker, stir and let the sauce heat through.*
12. *Serve hot over pasta.*

TIP
These meatballs make the ultimate sub.

TURKEY JOES

Makes 4 to 6 servings

Ingredients:

1⅓ pounds ground turkey breast

1 medium onion, minced

1 red bell pepper, chopped

1 teaspoon sea salt

½ teaspoon freshly ground pepper

⅓ cup brown sugar

½ teaspoon garlic powder

1 tablespoon Worcestershire sauce

1 tablespoon apple cider vinegar

3 tablespoons tomato paste

½ cup chicken stock

Whole-grain hamburger buns

Method:

1. *Place the turkey into the multi cooker.*
2. *Set to WHITE then cook and break apart the turkey using a rubber spatula until the turkey is browned.*
3. *Add remaining ingredients, except stock and buns, to the multi cooker; stir.*
4. *Secure lid and cook for 5 minutes.*
5. *Add the stock to the multi cooker; secure lid.*
6. *When multi cooker switches to KEEP WARM, serve on buns.*

WILD RICE
STUFFED PEPPERS

Makes 4 servings

Ingredients:

1 tablespoon extra-virgin olive oil

1 pound ground turkey breast

1 teaspoon salt

½ teaspoon freshly ground pepper

½ teaspoon garlic powder

1 medium onion, chopped

1 cup wild rice

4 cups chicken stock

½ cup mozzarella cheese, shredded

2 cups marinara sauce, divided

4 red bell peppers

Method:

1. *Pour oil into the multi cooker; set to WHITE and heat oil for 2 minutes.*
2. *Add the turkey, salt, pepper and garlic powder to the multi cooker.*
3. *Cook and break apart the turkey using a rubber spatula until browned.*
4. *Add the onions to the multi cooker; stir.*
5. *Secure the lid and cook for 2 minutes.*
6. *Add the rice and stock to the multi cooker; stir.*
7. *Secure lid and cook until the multi cooker switches to KEEP WARM.*
8. *Add the cheese and 1 cup of marinara sauce; stir.*
9. *Cut the tops off the bell peppers; discard the seeds and membranes.*
10. *Spoon the rice mixture into the bell peppers then place them into the multi cooker.*
11. *Top the peppers with remaining marinara sauce; secure lid.*
12. *Set to STEAM and timer to 15 minutes.*
13. *When cooking is complete, serve immediately.*

TURKEY
MEATLOAF

Makes 4 servings

Ingredients:

1 tablespoon unsalted butter

1 tablespoon extra-virgin olive oil

1 medium onion, chopped

8 ounces mushrooms, sliced

1 teaspoon salt

½ teaspoon freshly ground pepper

1 teaspoon fresh tarragon leaves, chopped

½ cup chicken stock

1 envelope unflavored gelatin

¼ cup rolled oats

2 large eggs, beaten

1 teaspoon Worcestershire sauce

½ cup Marsala wine

1½ pounds ground turkey breast

Method:

1. *Place the butter and oil into the multi cooker; secure lid.*

2. *Set to STEAM and timer to 15 minutes; let the butter melt for 1 minute.*

3. *Add the onions, secure lid and cook for 5 minutes.*

4. *Add the mushrooms, salt, pepper and tarragon to the multi cooker.*

5. *Secure lid and cook for an additional 2 minutes.*

6. *Turn off the multi cooker and let the mixture cool for 20 minutes.*

7. *Pour the chicken stock into a large bowl.*

8. *Sprinkle the gelatin over the stock and let rest for 1 minute.*

9. *Add the mushroom mixture and remaining ingredients to the bowl; gently combine by hand.*

10. *Pour 2 cups of water into the multi cooker.*

11. *Fit the multi cooker with the steamer basket.*

12. *Line the steamer basket with parchment paper then press the turkey mixture into the steamer basket; secure lid, set to WHITE and timer to 30 minutes.*

13. *When multi cooker switches to KEEP WARM, insert a meat thermometer into the center of the meatloaf to check if it registers 165°F. If not, continue to steam for 10 additional minutes or until the temperature is reached.*

14. *Serve immediately.*

TURKEY SAUSAGE &
PEPPERS

Makes 4 servings

Ingredients:

4 sweet Italian turkey sausage links

1 cup chicken stock

1 medium onion, thinly sliced

1 red bell pepper, julienned

4 whole grain hoagie rolls, toasted

Method:

1. *Place all ingredients, except rolls, into the multi cooker; stir then secure lid.*

2. *Set to STEAM and timer to 25 minutes.*

3. *When multi cooker switches to KEEP WARM, place the sausages on the rolls then top with onions and peppers.*

4. *Serve immediately.*

TIP
This is also amazing
served over your
favorite pasta.

LOW-FAT PASTA
BOLOGNESE

Makes 4 servings

Ingredients:

1 pound ground turkey

1 small onion, chopped

3 garlic cloves, minced

1 small carrot, peeled and diced

1 celery stalk, chopped

½ teaspoon salt

½ teaspoon freshly ground pepper

1½ cups chicken stock

1 can (28 ounces) crushed tomatoes

3 cups dry whole-grain pasta

1 teaspoon Italian herb seasoning

Method:

1. *Place the turkey into the multi cooker; set to WHITE.*
2. *Break turkey apart using a wooden spoon.*
3. *Close lid and cook for 10 minutes or until the turkey is cooked through.*
4. *Add the onions, garlic, carrots and celery to the multi cooker; stir.*
5. *Secure lid and cook for 5 minutes.*
6. *Add remaining ingredients to the multi cooker; stir then close lid.*
7. *When multi cooker switches to KEEP WARM, stir and serve.*

EASY SAUSAGE
SPAGHETTI SAUCE

Makes 6 to 8 servings

Ingredients:

2 pounds sweet Italian sausage, casings removed

10 garlic cloves, chopped

2 large white onions, chopped

Kosher salt and fresh pepper to taste

1 jar (28 ounces) tomato sauce

2 cans (6 ounces each) tomato paste

2 cups white wine or water

¼ cup ketchup

1 teaspoon anchovy paste (optional)

2 teaspoons dried oregano

1 teaspoon dried thyme

Method:

1. *Crumble the sausage into the multi cooker.*
2. *Set to STEAM and timer to 30 minutes.*
3. *Add the garlic and onions; stir occasionally until sausage is cooked through.*
4. *Drain any excess grease then add remaining ingredients; stir well then close lid.*
5. *When cooking is complete, adjust seasoning if desired.*
6. *Leave on KEEP WARM until ready to serve.*

HAM & GREENS
DINNER

Makes 6 servings

Ham & Greens Ingredients:

1½ pounds smoked ham chunks

7 cups pork or chicken stock

3 pounds turnip, collard or mustard greens, washed, trimmed and cut

Kosher salt and pepper to taste

Pepper sauce, for serving

Dumpling Ingredients:

1½ cups yellow cornmeal

1 teaspoon kosher salt

1 teaspoon black pepper

½ teaspoon baking powder

1 large egg

½ cup yellow onions, minced

⅔ cup water

Method:

1. *Place ham and stock into the multi cooker; set to STEAM and timer to 20 minutes.*
2. *When broth simmers, add greens by the handful and press them down until wilted.*
3. *Add remaining greens until all are wilted inside the multi cooker (they will all fit).*
4. *Season with salt and pepper.*
5. *Switch multi cooker to SLOW COOK and timer to 5 hours.*
6. *When 30 minutes remain on the timer, make the dumplings by stirring all dumpling ingredients together in a bowl.*
7. *Drop dumpling batter by small spoonfuls into the simmering greens; secure lid.*
8. *Let cook until the multi cooker switches to KEEP WARM.*
9. *Serve hot in bowls with pepper sauce.*

SLOW & EASY
PULLED PORK

Makes 6 servings

ENTREES

Ingredients:

4 pounds pork shoulder

2 bottles (12 ounces each) root beer or cola

1 cup ketchup

½ cup yellow mustard

2 teaspoons kosher salt

1 teaspoon black pepper

½ teaspoon chili flakes

Soft buns, for serving

Coleslaw, for serving

Method:

1. *Place all ingredients, except buns and coleslaw, into the multi cooker; stir and secure lid.*
2. *Set to SLOW COOK and timer to 6 hours.*
3. *When cooking is complete, skim off excess fat from the surface.*
4. *Shred meat using tongs then adjust seasoning if desired.*
5. *Serve on buns with coleslaw on the side.*

TIP

You can make the root beer flavor even more pronounced by adding 1/2 teaspoon of root beer concentrate, which you can find in the spice aisle of your grocery store.

SHREDDED
PORK TACOS

Makes 6 to 8 servings

Ingredients:

4 pounds pork shoulder

8 garlic cloves, minced

1 large white onion, sliced

2 tablespoons powdered pork or chicken bouillon

Kosher salt and pepper to taste

1 teaspoon dried thyme

2 teaspoons dried coriander

2 teaspoons ground cumin

1 teaspoon oregano

½ cup whole milk

1 cup water

Corn or flour tortillas

Method:

1. *Place all ingredients, except tortillas, into the multi cooker; stir then secure lid.*
2. *Set to SLOW COOK and timer to 6 hours.*
3. *When multi cooker switches to KEEP WARM, remove the meat.*
4. *Skim excess fat from the surface of the liquid inside the multi cooker.*
5. *Using a pair of tongs and a fork, shred the pork into long, thin strands.*
6. *Return the shredded meat to the multi cooker and stir well.*
7. *Adjust seasoning if desired then serve on tortillas.*

TIP

Serve with your favorite toppings such as
shredded green cabbage, shredded cheese, salsa,
sliced purple onions, chopped cilantro and sliced avocado.

HAMBURGER CASSEROLE

Makes 6 servings

Ingredients:

1 package (32 ounces) frozen potato tots, thawed and divided

1 pound ground beef

1 large yellow onion, chopped

4 garlic cloves, minced

2 cans (10.75 ounces each) cream of chicken soup

1 cup whole milk

1 cup Cheddar cheese, shredded

Method:

1. *Pour half of the potato tots into the multi cooker and press them into a layer.*
2. *Set to SLOW COOK and timer to 4 hours.*
3. *In a skillet over medium heat, combine the ground beef, onions and garlic.*
4. *Cook for 10 minutes, stirring occasionally, or until beef is browned.*
5. *Drain excess grease then add the soup and milk to the skillet; stir until combined.*
6. *Stir in the cheese and mix thoroughly.*
7. *Pour the beef mixture into the multi cooker over the potato tots.*
8. *Top beef mixture with remaining potato tots; secure lid.*
9. *When cooking is complete, serve immediately.*

TIP

When serving, cut the casserole so that each serving has potatoes from top to bottom.

BRAISED ROAST BEEF & VEGGIES

Makes 6 servings

Ingredients:

1 tablespoon canola oil

3 pounds eye-of-round beef roast, tied

Kosher salt and fresh pepper to taste

½ cup red wine or water

3 bay leaves

3 sprigs fresh thyme

3 Russet potatoes, cut into cubes

3 carrots, peeled and chunked

1 large onion, chunked

3 celery stalks, chunked

1 cup tomato juice

3 cups beef stock

2 tablespoons quick-cook tapioca

Method:

1. *Preheat the oil in a large skillet over medium-high heat.*

2. *When oil is hot, add the roast to the skillet; season with salt and pepper.*

3. *Sear beef on all sides until brown then transfer to the multi cooker.*

4. *Add the wine to the skillet to deglaze; scrape up all the brown bits from the bottom of the pan then transfer to the multi cooker.*

5. *Add remaining ingredients to the multi cooker; stir to distribute the tapioca.*

6. *Secure lid, set to SLOW COOK and timer to 8 hours.*

7. *When multi cooker switches to KEEP WARM taste and adjust seasoning if desired.*

8. *Remove the roast, cut the string then pull it into serving-size pieces.*

9. *Serve the roast with the vegetables and gravy.*

EASY ON THE BUDGET
SWISS STEAK

Makes 6 servings

Ingredients:

2 pounds round steaks, cut into 6 pieces and pounded thin

2 large onions, sliced

1 green bell pepper, sliced

2 celery stalks, sliced

2 carrots, peeled and sliced

2 cans (14.5 ounces each) stewed tomatoes

4 tablespoons all purpose flour

1 teaspoon kosher salt

1 teaspoon black pepper

3 garlic cloves, minced

1 tablespoon powdered beef bouillon

Hot cooked noodles, for serving

Method:

1. *Layer the steak, onions, peppers, celery and carrots inside the multi cooker.*
2. *In a bowl, combine remaining ingredients, except noodles; whisk well.*
3. *Pour mixture over the ingredients in the multi cooker; stir slightly then secure lid.*
4. *Set to SLOW COOK and timer to 4 hours.*
5. *When cooking is complete, adjust seasoning if desired.*
6. *Serve over a bed of hot noodles.*

TIP

To save time, you can buy cubed beef steak at the grocery store that is already tenderized and pounded thin.

ENTREES

MOROCCAN CHICKEN

Makes 4 servings

Ingredients:

1 tablespoon extra-virgin olive oil

1 medium onion, chopped

3 garlic cloves, minced

4 boneless, skinless chicken breasts

1 teaspoon tumeric powder

6 saffron strands

1 teaspoon salt, or to taste

2 whole preserved lemons (see recipe on page 136)

½ cup black olives, sliced

2 cups chicken stock

2 tablespoons fresh cilantro leaves, chopped

Method:

1. *Pour oil into the multi cooker; set to WHITE and heat oil for 2 minutes.*
2. *Add the onions and garlic to the multi cooker.*
3. *Secure lid and cook for 5 minutes.*
4. *Add the chicken, tumeric, saffron and salt to the multi cooker.*
5. *Secure lid and cook for 5 minutes.*
6. *Open lid, turn the chicken breasts then add the lemons, olives and stock.*
7. *Secure lid and cook for 20 minutes.*
8. *Top with cilantro and serve.*

TIP
Serve the chicken over couscous.

THAI GREEN CHICKEN CURRY

Makes 4 servings

Ingredients:

2 tablespoons extra-virgin olive oil

4 boneless, skinless chicken breasts, cut into thin strips

1⅔ cups light coconut milk

2 tablespoons green curry paste

3 tablespoons Thai fish sauce

1 teaspoon lime zest

1 red bell pepper, seeds removed, cut into thin strips

1 carrot, peeled and sliced ½-inch thick

1 cup sugar snap peas

8 basil leaves, torn

Method:

1. *Pour oil into the multi cooker; set to WHITE and heat oil for 2 minutes.*
2. *Add the chicken, stir and cook for 8 minutes or until cooked through.*
3. *Transfer the chicken to a plate; set aside.*
4. *Add the coconut milk and curry paste to the multi cooker; stir then secure lid.*
5. *Set to WHITE and cook for 3 minutes.*
6. *Add the fish sauce, lime zest, peppers and carrots to the multi cooker.*
7. *Secure lid and cook for 4 minutes.*
8. *Add remaining ingredients to the multi cooker.*
9. *Secure lid and cook for an additional 10 minutes.*
10. *Serve over the chicken.*

TIP

Serve over a bed of
hot jasmine rice topped
with chopped cilantro.

STUFFED CHICKEN WITH ORZO

Makes 2 to 4 servings

Ingredients:

4 thin chicken cutlets

2 tablespoons Dijon mustard

1 pound Swiss chard, washed and chopped

4 Brie cheese slices

½ teaspoon salt

Pinch of freshly ground pepper

2 tablespoons extra-virgin olive oil

1 cup orzo

1 cup chicken stock

1 can (14.5 ounces) diced tomatoes

¼ cup fresh parsley, chopped

1 tablespoon unsalted butter

1 tablespoon lemon juice

Method:

1. *Place the chicken on a cutting board and spread the mustard over the chicken.*
2. *Top the chicken with Swiss chard, Brie, salt and pepper.*
3. *Roll each cutlet tightly then secure each roll with a toothpick.*
4. *Pour oil into the multi cooker; set to STEAM and timer to 15 minutes.*
5. *Heat oil for 2 minutes then place the chicken, toothpick-side up, into the multi cooker.*
6. *Cook for 3 minutes on both sides then transfer the chicken to a platter.*
7. *Add the orzo and stock to the multi cooker.*
8. *Fit the multi cooker with the steamer basket.*
9. *Place the chicken into the steamer basket; secure lid and set to WHITE.*
10. *When multi cooker switches to KEEP WARM, remove the steamer basket and set aside.*
11. *Add remaining ingredients to the multi cooker; stir.*
12. *Remove the toothpicks from the chicken and slice diagonally.*
13. *Transfer the multi cooker contents to a platter, top with chicken and serve.*

STEAMED CHICKEN

Makes 4 servings

Ingredients:

4 small boneless, skinless chicken breasts

¼ teaspoon salt

¼ teaspoon freshly ground pepper

2 tablespoons soy sauce

1 teaspoon rice wine vinegar

1 teaspoon honey

1 teaspoon sesame oil

1 tablespoon cornstarch

1 tablespoon ginger, grated

1 green onion, chopped

2 cups basmati rice, rinsed

2 cups chicken stock

Method:

1. *In a large bowl, combine all ingredients, except rice and stock.*
2. *Let marinate for 20 minutes.*
3. *Place the rice and stock into the multi cooker.*
4. *Fit the multi cooker with the steamer basket.*
5. *Transfer the chicken from the bowl to the steamer basket.*
6. *Secure lid and set to WHITE.*
7. *When multi cooker switches to KEEP WARM, serve immediately.*

BUDGET
CHICKEN CURRY

Makes 6 servings

Ingredients:

2 tablespoons butter or ghee

2 tablespoons fresh ginger, minced

1 tablespoon fresh garlic, minced

1 large yellow onion, chopped

2 tablespoons curry powder

1 tablespoon all purpose flour

3 tablespoons Thai red curry paste

1 family pack chicken drumsticks

4 cups chicken stock

1 cup unsweetened coconut milk

Juice of a lime

2 teaspoons honey

Kosher salt to taste

Method:

1. *Add butter or ghee to the multi cooker; set to STEAM and timer to 15 minutes.*
2. *Add the ginger, garlic and onions to the multi cooker; stir until fragrant.*
3. *Add the curry powder, flour and curry paste; stir well and sauté until fragrant.*
4. *Add remaining ingredients to the multi cooker; secure lid.*
5. *Switch multi cooker to SLOW COOK and set timer to 4 hours.*
6. *When cooking is complete, adjust seasoning if desired and serve.*

TIP
This dish is best served with steamed rice, cilantro sprigs and plain yogurt.

CHICKEN NOODLE-O
DINNER

Makes 4 to 6 servings

Ingredients:

4 boneless, skinless chicken thighs, cubed

3 carrots, peeled and sliced

2 celery stalks, sliced

1 large onion, diced

½ teaspoon dried sage

½ teaspoon dried thyme

4 cups flavorful chicken stock (add bouillon if desired)

1 cup whole milk

Kosher salt and fresh pepper to taste

4 cups ring pasta, dry

1 cup frozen peas

Method:

1. *Place all ingredients, except peas, into the multi cooker; stir.*
2. *Secure lid and set to WHITE.*
3. *When multi cooker switches to KEEP WARM, adjust seasoning if desired.*
4. *Stir in the peas and let rest for 5 minutes.*
5. *Serve hot in bowls.*

TIP
You can substitute
the chicken with
ham, pork or beef.

ASIAN NOODLES WITH SHRIMP

Makes 4 servings

Ingredients:

1 package (6.75 ounces) rice stick noodles

⅔ cup water

4 tablespoons fresh lime juice

3 tablespoons fish sauce

4 teaspoons chili-garlic sauce

2 teaspoons sugar

1 pound medium shrimp, peeled and deveined

2 cups sugar snap peas, cut crosswise

1 red bell pepper, thinly sliced

1 cup Japanese or English cucumbers, thinly sliced

½ cup fresh mint leaves, chopped

½ cup fresh cilantro leaves, chopped

Method:

1. *Place the noodles, water, lime juice, fish sauce, chili sauce, sugar and shrimp into the multi cooker; stir.*

2. *Fit the multi cooker with the steamer basket.*

3. *Place the snap peas and peppers into the steamer basket.*

4. *Secure lid and set to WHITE.*

5. *When multi cooker switches to KEEP WARM transfer the multi cooker contents to a plate and let cool.*

6. *Add remaining ingredients to the plate, stir and serve chilled.*

TIP

Most of these ingredients are readily found in your grocery store's Asian section.

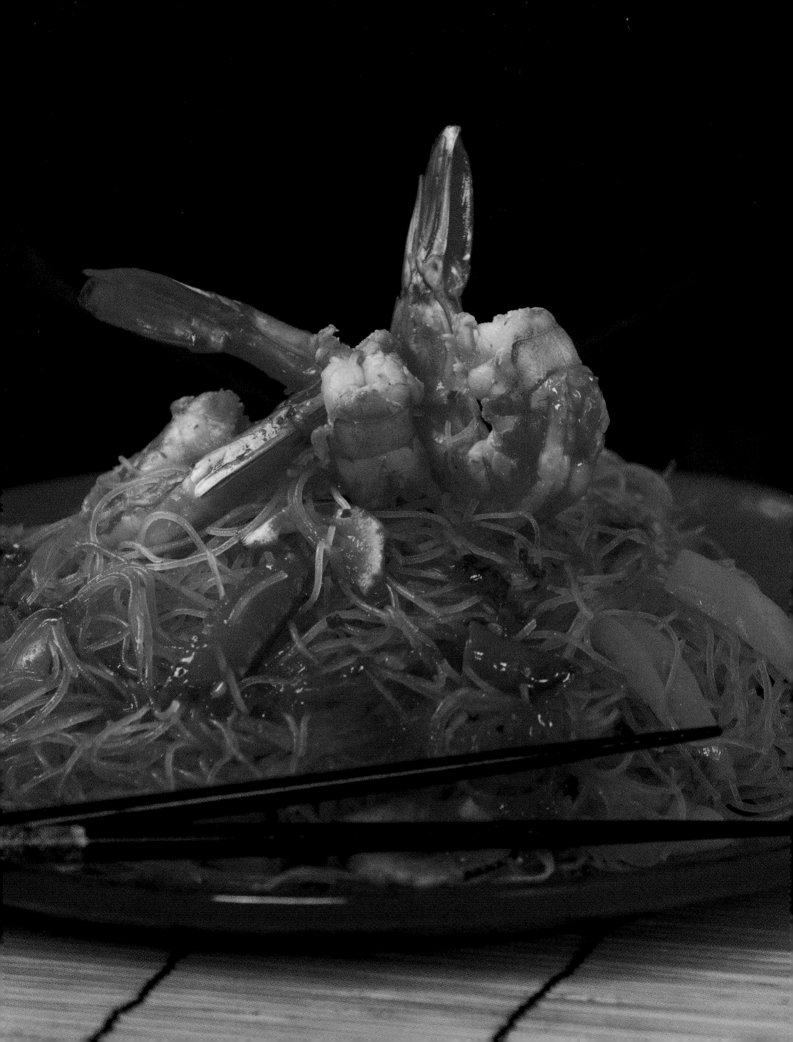

SHRIMP PASTA
PRIMAVERA

Makes 4 servings

Ingredients:

2 cups dry penne pasta

2 cups chicken stock

1 shallot, minced

2 garlic cloves, minced

½ teaspoon salt

½ teaspoon freshly ground pepper

1 pound medium shrimp, peeled and deveined

½ cup fresh corn kernels

½ cup zucchini, sliced

¼ cup peas

2 ounces low-fat cream cheese

2 tablespoons low-fat milk

2 tablespoons Parmesan cheese, grated

Method:

1. *Place the pasta, stock, shallots, garlic, salt and pepper into the multi cooker; stir.*
2. *Secure lid, set to WHITE and cook for 15 minutes.*
3. *Stir in the shrimp and corn.*
4. *Secure lid and cook for an additional 10 minutes.*
5. *Add remaining ingredients to the multi cooker; stir well until the cheese is melted.*
6. *Serve immediately.*

SHRIMP ARRABBIATA

Makes 4 servings

ENTREES

Ingredients:

2 tablespoons extra-virgin olive oil

1 medium onion, minced

3 garlic cloves, minced

1 teaspoon salt

½ teaspoon freshly ground pepper

½ teaspoon crushed red pepper flakes

1 jar (28 ounces) pasta sauce

1½ cups chicken stock

1½ cups whole wheat dried pasta

1 pound shrimp, peeled and deveined

5 fresh basil leaves, chopped

Method:

1. *Pour oil into the multi cooker; set to WHITE and heat oil for 2 minutes.*
2. *Add the onions to the multi cooker.*
3. *Secure lid and cook for 5 minutes.*
4. *Add remaining ingredients, except shrimp and basil, to the multi cooker; stir.*
5. *Secure lid and cook for 20 minutes.*
6. *Add the shrimp to the multi cooker.*
7. *Secure lid and cook for an additional 10 minutes.*
8. *Top with basil and serve.*

SHRIMP SCAMPI

Makes 4 servings

Ingredients:

1 package (9 ounces) fresh linguine pasta

½ cup chicken stock

½ cup white wine

3 garlic cloves, minced

1 shallot, minced

1 pound jumbo shrimp, peeled and deveined

½ teaspoon salt

½ teaspoon freshly ground pepper

½ teaspoon garlic powder

¼ cup butter

2 tablespoons pesto (see recipe on page 138)

¼ teaspoon crushed red pepper flakes

Method:

1. *Place the pasta, stock, wine, garlic and shallots into the multi cooker; stir.*
2. *Season the shrimp with salt, pepper and garlic powder.*
3. *Fit multi cooker with the steamer basket.*
4. *Place the shrimp into the steamer basket; secure lid.*
5. *Set to STEAM and timer to 15 minutes.*
6. *When cooking is complete, transfer the shrimp from the steamer basket to the pasta in the bottom of the multi cooker.*
7. *Add remaining ingredients to the multi cooker, stir and serve.*

MUSSELS IN SPICY TOMATO SAUCE

Makes 4 servings

Ingredients:

1 tablespoon extra-virgin olive oil

1 medium onion, chopped

3 garlic cloves, minced

1 teaspoon salt

½ teaspoon freshly ground pepper

½ teaspoon crushed red pepper flakes

1 pound mussels, cleaned with beards removed

1 can (28 ounces) fire roasted tomatoes

¼ cup white wine

2 tablespoons fresh parsley, chopped

Method:

1. *Pour oil into the multi cooker; set to STEAM and timer to 20 minutes.*
2. *Heat oil for 2 minutes then add the onions to the multi cooker.*
3. *Sauté for 5 minutes or until onions are softened.*
4. *Add the garlic, salt, pepper and pepper flakes to the multi cooker; stir.*
5. *Cook for 1 minute then add remaining ingredients, except parsley.*
6. *Secure lid and cook for an additional 10 minutes.*
7. *Top with parsley and serve.*

TIP

This is the ultimate appetizer or a perfect main dish over pasta.

SHELLS WITH RED CLAM SAUCE

Makes 4 servings

Ingredients:

2 cans (10 ounces each) whole baby clams

3 cups dry shell-shaped pasta

1 cup chicken stock

1 can (14 ounces) petite diced tomatoes

3 garlic cloves, minced

½ teaspoon crushed red pepper flakes

6 whole littleneck clams, in the shell

1 sprig fresh thyme

2 tablespoons fresh parsley, chopped

Method:

1. *Drain the juice from the clams into the multi cooker; reserve the clams.*
2. *Add the pasta, stock, tomatoes and garlic to the multi cooker; stir then secure lid.*
3. *Set to WHITE and cook for 15 minutes.*
4. *Add remaining ingredients, except parsley, to the multi cooker; stir.*
5. *Secure lid and cook for an additional 5 minutes.*
6. *Remove thyme sprig and serve.*

LOBSTER ALFREDO

Makes 4 servings

Ingredients:

1 package (9 ounces) fresh fettuccine pasta

1 cup chicken stock

1 cup white wine

2 garlic cloves, minced

1 teaspoon salt

½ teaspoon freshly ground pepper

1 cup cooked lobster meat

2 tablespoons unsalted butter

½ cup heavy cream

¼ cup Romano cheese, grated

1 tablespoon fresh parsley, chopped

Method:

1. *Place the pasta, stock, wine, garlic, salt and pepper into the multi cooker; stir.*
2. *Secure lid and set to WHITE.*
3. *When multi cooker switches to KEEP WARM, add remaining ingredients and stir until cheese is melted.*
4. *Serve immediately.*

TIP
Fresh pasta can be found in the refrigerated section of your grocery store.

CALIFORNIA ROLL

Makes 4 to 6 servings

Sushi Rice Ingredients:

2 cups short grain rice, rinsed

2 cups water

3 tablespoons rice wine vinegar

1 teaspoon salt

1 tablespoon sugar

Sushi Roll Ingredients:

5 nori sheets (seaweed)

1 medium cucumber, peeled and cut lengthwise into ¼-inch pieces

1 avocado, peeled, pitted and thinly sliced

½ cup crab meat

1 tablespoon rice wine vinegar

Method:

1. *Place all sushi rice ingredients into the multi cooker.*
2. *Secure lid and set to WHITE.*
3. *When multi cooker switches to KEEP WARM, transfer the rice to a platter; let cool.*
4. *To assemble sushi roll, place a sheet of nori, shiny-side down, on a bamboo mat.*
5. *Spread 1 scoop of rice across the nori, leaving a 1-inch band without rice.*
6. *Arrange the cucumber, avocado and crab meat on the rice opposite of the band.*
7. *Roll tightly to cover the filling.*
8. *Rub vinegar on the band of the nori and roll tightly; hold together for 10 seconds.*
9. *Cut roll into 6 slices and serve.*

TIP

Serve this roll with wasabi, soy sauce and sliced pickled ginger.

SALMON & VODKA
ORECCHIETTE

Makes 2 to 4 servings

Ingredients:

2 cups dry orecchiette pasta

1 cup chicken stock

1 can (14 ounces) petite diced tomatoes

1 shallot, minced

3 garlic cloves, minced

2 tablespoons pesto (see recipe on page 138)

2 large salmon fillets

2 cups baby spinach leaves

2 ounces low-fat cream cheese

¼ cup low-fat milk

¼ cup vodka

¼ cup Parmesan cheese, grated

1 teaspoon salt

½ teaspoon freshly ground pepper

Method:

1. *Place the pasta, stock, tomatoes, shallots and garlic into the multi cooker; stir.*
2. *Spread the pesto over the salmon fillets.*
3. *Fit the multi cooker with the steamer basket and place the spinach into the basket.*
4. *Place the salmon over the spinach; secure lid.*
5. *Set to STEAM and timer to 10 minutes.*
6. *When cooking is complete, remove the steamer basket and set aside.*
7. *Add the cream cheese and milk to the multi cooker; stir then secure lid.*
8. *Set to STEAM and timer to 10 minutes.*
9. *When cooking is complete, add the vodka, Parmesan cheese, salt and pepper to the multi cooker; stir.*
10. *Cut salmon into pieces and serve with spinach on a bed of pasta.*

CHILI GINGER
TILAPIA

Makes 2 servings

Ingredients:

3 tablespoons chili-garlic sauce

1 tablespoon fresh ginger, grated

1 tablespoon lime juice

1 teaspoon soy sauce

1 teaspoon honey

1 cup sugar snap peas

1 red bell pepper, julienned

2 tilapia fillets (4 ounces each)

1 cup jasmine rice, rinsed

1 cup chicken stock

Method:

1. *In a bowl, combine chili sauce, ginger, lime juice, soy sauce and honey; mix well.*
2. *Place snap peas, peppers and tilapia into the honey mixture; cover and refrigerate for 1 hour.*
3. *Place the rice and stock into the multi cooker; secure lid.*
4. *Set to WHITE and cook for 10 minutes.*
5. *Open lid and fit the multi cooker with the steamer basket.*
6. *Add the bowl contents from the refrigerator to the steamer basket; secure lid.*
7. *When multi cooker switches to KEEP WARM, serve immediately.*

TIP

Tilapia is so mild in taste that if you serve it to people who claim they don't like fish, they are usually quite surprised!

BREAKFAST BERRY COUSCOUS

Makes 2 to 4 servings

Ingredients:

1 cup couscous

1½ cups cranberry juice

3 cups fresh berries

1 teaspoon agave syrup

1 cup plain yogurt (optional)

Method:

1. *Place the couscous and cranberry juice into the multi cooker.*
2. *Secure lid and set to WHITE.*
3. *When multi cooker switches to KEEP WARM, fluff the couscous using a fork.*
4. *Add remaining ingredients, stir and serve in bowls.*

TIP

If you don't have agave syrup, you can substitute it with a teaspoon of honey.

BLUEBERRY CRISP

Makes 4 servings

Ingredients:

1 cup unbleached all purpose flour

¼ cup brown sugar

1 teaspoon baking powder

1 teaspoon vanilla extract

½ cup (1 stick) unsalted butter, melted

2 large eggs, beaten

1 cup plain yogurt

4 cups frozen blueberries

¼ cup sugar

1 tablespoon lemon juice

½ cup granola cereal

Method:

1. *In a large bowl, combine flour, brown sugar, baking powder, vanilla, butter, eggs and yogurt; mix until slightly lumpy.*

2. *Place the blueberries, sugar and lemon juice into the multi cooker.*

3. *Pour the batter into the multi cooker and top with granola; secure lid.*

4. *Set to STEAM and timer to 30 minutes.*

5. *When multi cooker switches to KEEP WARM, let rest for 20 minutes before serving.*

TIP

To make it extra special, serve this topped with vanilla ice cream.

DUMPLINGS IN BERRY SAUCE

Makes 4 to 6 servings

Dumplings:

1 cup unbleached all purpose flour

1½ teaspoons baking powder

¼ cup sugar

2 tablespoons unsalted butter, softened

⅓ cup milk

1 teaspoon vanilla extract

Pinch of allspice

Fruit Sauce:

3 tablespoons cornstarch

2 cups water

4 cups fresh berries

¾ cup sugar

4 tablespoons unsalted butter, melted

¼ teaspoon salt

Pinch of allspice

Method:

1. *In a bowl, combine all dumpling ingredients; mix well then set aside.*
2. *Dissolve the cornstarch in the water then pour the cornstarch mixture into the multi cooker.*
3. *Add remaining fruit sauce ingredients to the multi cooker; stir then secure lid.*
4. *Set to STEAM and timer to 20 minutes.*
5. *After 10 minutes of cooking, drop the dumpling mixture by tablespoons into the multi cooker; secure lid.*
6. *When multi cooker switches to KEEP WARM, let rest inside the multi cooker for 15 minutes before serving.*

TIP

Serve this in a bowl with your favorite ice cream topped with whipped cream.

BANANA RUM BREAD PUDDING

Makes 4 servings

Ingredients:

4 cups challah bread, diced into 1-inch cubes

Butter-flavored non-stick spray

1 cup golden raisins

2 tablespoons dark rum

6 large eggs, beaten

2 cups heavy cream

1 cup sugar

1 teaspoon vanilla extract

1 teaspoon pumpkin pie spice

4 ripe bananas, sliced

Method:

1. *Preheat oven to 350 degrees.*
2. *Place the bread cubes on a baking sheet and spray with butter-flavored non-stick cooking spray.*
3. *Bake in the oven for 10 minutes; remove and set aside.*
4. *In a bowl, soak the raisins in rum.*
5. *In a separate bowl, combine the eggs, cream and sugar; mix well.*
6. *Add the vanilla and pumpkin pie spice to the egg mixture; mix well.*
7. *Add the raisin mixture and banana slices to the egg mixture.*
8. *Add the bread cubes to the egg mixture; let soak for 5 minutes.*
9. *Pour the entire mixture into the multi cooker; secure lid.*
10. *Set to STEAM and timer to 30 minutes.*
11. *When cooking is complete, let rest on KEEP WARM for 20 minutes before serving.*

TIP

Serve this with the banana salsa on page 141.

LOW-FAT
BREAD PUDDING

Makes 4 to 6 servings

SWEETS

Ingredients:

1 multi-grain baguette, cut into 1-inch cubes

Butter-flavored non-stick spray

4 cups low-fat milk

1 cup egg substitute

¾ cup sugar

1 teaspoon vanilla extract

1 teaspoon ground cinnamon

½ teaspoon ground nutmeg

Method:

1. *Preheat oven to 350 degrees.*
2. *Place the bread cubes on a baking sheet and spray with butter-flavored non-stick cooking spray.*
3. *Bake in the oven for 10 minutes; remove and set aside.*
4. *In a large bowl, combine remaining ingredients; beat well using a whisk.*
5. *Add the bread cubes to the bowl; let soak for 15 minutes.*
6. *Pour the mixture into the multi cooker; secure lid.*
7. *Set to STEAM and timer to 30 minutes.*
8. *When cooking is complete, let rest on KEEP WARM for 20 minutes before serving.*
9. *Serve hot topped with maple syrup or fruit compote.*

TIP
For a twist,
add 1/2 cup of raisins
before cooking.

PUMPKIN PUDDING

Makes 4 servings

Ingredients:

2 large eggs, beaten
2 cups canned pumpkin
1 cup brown sugar
1 cup evaporated milk
2 teaspoons pumpkin pie spice
Pinch of salt
2 cups water

Method:

1. *In a bowl, combine all ingredients, except water; mix well.*
2. *Apply non-stick spray to 4 ramekins.*
3. *Divide the bowl contents between the 4 ramekins.*
4. *Wrap each ramekin in aluminum foil.*
5. *Pour the water into the multi cooker to create a water bath.*
6. *Stack the ramekins inside the multi cooker; secure lid.*
7. *Set to STEAM and timer to 25 minutes.*
8. *When cooking is complete, let cool to room temperature before serving.*

TIP
Top with
ice cream and
whipped topping.

CHILLY RICE PUDDING

Makes 4 servings

SWEETS

Ingredients:

1 cup rice, cooked

2 cups half & half

1 cup sugar, divided

1 vanilla bean, split in half

4 large egg yolks

1 cup whipped topping

Method:

1. *Place rice, half & half, 1/2 cup of sugar and the vanilla bean into the multi cooker.*

2. *Secure lid and set to WHITE.*

3. *Cook for 15 minutes then manually switch the multi cooker to KEEP WARM.*

4. *In a bowl, combine remaining sugar and egg yolks.*

5. *Add 1 tablespoon of the rice mixture to the egg mixture; stir.*

6. *Pour the egg mixture into the multi cooker and stir for 1 minute.*

7. *Remove the vanilla bean and scrape the seeds from the vanilla bean into the rice mixture using a sharp knife; stir.*

8. *Transfer the rice mixture to a bowl and refrigerate for 1 hour.*

9. *Fold in the whipped topping and serve.*

TIP

Dust with cinnamon
and brown sugar
before serving.

ORANGE TAPIOCA PUDDING

Makes 6 to 8 servings

Ingredients:

1 cup tapioca pearls

½ cup sugar

5 cups water, divided

2 oranges, peeled and sectioned

1 tablespoon fresh orange zest

Method:

1. *In a bowl, combine the tapioca, sugar and 1 cup of water; let soak for 2 hours.*
2. *Pour the tapioca and remaining ingredients into the multi cooker; stir.*
3. *Secure lid and set to WHITE.*
4. *When multi cooker switches to KEEP WARM, transfer the pudding to a bowl and refrigerate until ready to serve.*

THICK & CREAMY
HOT CHOCOLATE

Makes 8 servings

SWEETS

Ingredients:

6 cups whole milk

2 cups half & half

⅓ cup granulated sugar

2½ cups good quality dark chocolate pieces

2 teaspoons vanilla extract

Small pinch of kosher salt

Marshmallows, for serving

Method:

1. *Pour the milk, half & half and sugar into the multi cooker; keep lid open.*

2. *Set to STEAM and timer to 20 minutes.*

3. *When mixture begins to simmer, switch the multi cooker to KEEP WARM.*

4. *Whisk in the chocolate, vanilla and salt until completely smooth.*

5. *Serve in mugs topped with marshmallows.*

TIP

For peppermint hot chocolate,
simply add a candy cane
to each mug before serving.

STRAWBERRY CREAM CHEESE MINIS

Makes 6 servings

Ingredients:

6 large strawberries, stems removed

4 ounces cream cheese, softened

3 tablespoons granulated sugar

1⅓ cups half & half

4 large egg yolks

1 large egg

1½ cups hot water

SWEETS

Method:

1. *Place the strawberries, cream cheese and sugar into a blender; purée until smooth.*

2. *Add remaining ingredients, except water; purée for an additional 5 seconds.*

3. *Apply non-stick spray to 6 small decorative molds or ramekins.*

4. *Divide the mixture between the molds; cover the top of each mold with aluminum foil.*

5. *Pour the water into the multi cooker to create a water bath.*

6. *Set to STEAM and timer to 25 minutes.*

7. *Place 3 molds into the bottom of the multi cooker.*

8. *Fit the multi cooker with the steamer basket then place remaining molds into the basket; secure lid.*

9. *Cook for 20-25 minutes or until centers are just wobbly; do not overcook.*

10. *Remove immediately.*

11. *Chill for several hours before removing the foil and inverting onto a serving dish.*

TIP

Be sure to use small molds for this recipe so they all fit inside the multi cooker.

LIGHT
CHEESECAKE

Makes 3 servings

Ingredients:

1 package (8 ounces) low-fat cream cheese

⅓ cup sugar

¼ cup egg substitute

¼ cup low-fat sour cream

½ teaspoon cornstarch

½ teaspoon vanilla extract

1 cup water

Method:

1. *Using a food processor, process the cream cheese and sugar until smooth.*

2. *Add remaining ingredients, except water; process for an additional minute.*

3. *Cut round pieces of parchment paper to fit the bottom of three 4-ounce ramekins.*

4. *Place a parchment piece into each ramekin and apply non-stick spray.*

5. *Fill each ramekin with batter then wrap in aluminum foil.*

6. *Pour the water into the multi cooker to create a water bath.*

7. *Stack the ramekins inside the multi cooker; secure lid.*

8. *Set to STEAM and timer to 25 minutes.*

9. *When cooking is complete, chill for 2 hours.*

10. *To serve, run a knife along the edges of the ramekins then invert the cheesecakes onto plates.*

OLD FASHIONED
CUP CUSTARD

Makes 4 servings

Ingredients:

1½ cups half & half
1 small vanilla bean, split
¼ cup sugar
2 egg yolks
1 large egg
Pinch of nutmeg

Method:

1. *Place the half & half and the vanilla bean into the multi cooker; secure lid.*
2. *Set to STEAM and timer to 5 minutes.*
3. *In a bowl, combine sugar, egg yolks and egg; mix until sugar is dissolved.*
4. *When cooking is complete, remove the multi cooker insert using an oven mitt and slowly pour the half & half mixture into the bowl with the egg mixture while whisking.*
5. *Pour the mixture through a sieve into another bowl to remove any curdles.*
6. *Scrape the seeds from the vanilla bean into the strained mixture.*
7. *Rinse the multi cooker insert and place it back into the multi cooker.*
8. *Pour 1/2 cup of water into the multi cooker to create a water bath.*
9. *Apply non-stick spray to 4 ramekins.*
10. *Divide the mixture between the ramekins and top each ramekin with nutmeg.*
11. *Wrap each ramekin in aluminum foil and stack them inside the multi cooker.*
12. *Secure lid, set to STEAM and timer to 30 minutes.*
13. *When cooking is complete, serve hot or cold.*

PRESERVED LEMONS

Makes 6 to 8 servings

Ingredients:

8 lemons, scrubbed and ends removed
8 teaspoons sea salt
Lemon juice

Method:

1. *Place the lemons vertically on a cutting board.*
2. *Using a knife, make 2 incisions that go 2/3 through the lemon to form an X shape.*
3. *Sprinkle 1 teaspoon of salt into each lemon.*
4. *Pack the lemons tightly into a large, sterilized glass container with a lid.*
5. *Fill the container to the top with lemon juice and close the lid.*
6. *Let sit on the counter for 5 weeks.*
7. *Serve over Moroccan dishes like couscous or stew.*

TIP
Purchase lemons
with thin skin as they
are much tastier.

EASY
PESTO
Makes 1 cup

Ingredients:

2 garlic cloves

3 tablespoons unsalted butter

½ teaspoon freshly ground pepper

½ cup Parmesan cheese, grated

2 cups basil leaves

⅓ cup spinach leaves

¼ cup extra-virgin olive oil

Method:

1. *Place all ingredients, except oil, into a food processor.*
2. *With the food processor running, slowly drizzle oil through the feed tube into the food processor.*
3. *Serve over your favorite meat or fish.*

SALSA VERDE

Makes 6 to 8 servings

Ingredients:

2 Poblano chile peppers, seeds and membranes removed

8 tomatillos, husks removed

1 garlic clove, minced

1 small onion, quartered

2 cups chicken stock

1 teaspoon cumin seeds

1 teaspoon salt

¼ cup fresh cilantro leaves

1 tablespoon fresh lime juice

Method:

1. *Place all ingredients, except cilantro and lime juice, into the multi cooker; stir.*
2. *Secure lid, set to STEAM and timer to 20 minutes.*
3. *When cooking is complete, let cool then transfer to a food processor.*
4. *Add remaining ingredients to the food processor; purée until smooth and serve.*

RASPBERRY SAUCE

Makes 2 to 4 servings

Ingredients:

1 bag (12 ounces) frozen raspberries

⅓ cup sugar

2 teaspoons lemon juice

Method:

1. *Place all ingredients into the multi cooker; stir then secure lid.*

2. *Set to STEAM and timer to 10 minutes.*

3. *When multi cooker switches to KEEP WARM, pour sauce through a sieve and serve.*

TIP

This is delicious served
over the light cheesecake
on page 134.

BANANA
SALSA

Makes 6 servings

Ingredients:

3 tablespoons unsalted butter

3 tablespoons brown sugar

¼ cup dark rum

¼ cup orange juice

3 firm bananas, diced

Method:

1. *Place all ingredients into the multi cooker; stir then secure lid.*
2. *Set to STEAM and timer to 10 minutes.*
3. *When cooking is complete, serve over your favorite ice cream.*

TIP

This is incredible served over the Banana Rum Bread Pudding on page 124.